PRIME

ANURADHA SRIVASTAVA

ISBN 979-888546446-8

Prime

<u>Prime Review</u> – Single Click App Drives Free Traffic From 300 Sources.

Prime is the world's 1st 7-in-1 multi-channel traffic app that drives free buyer traffic.

The sources are...

Social Media.

SMS.

Facebook Messenger.

Email.

Push Notifications.

Video Sites.

Automated LIVE Streams.

<u>Visit My Official Website</u>

Enter Caption

Combined with these channels, there are almost 4 billion users. And think if you could click a button to send traffic to any link to 300 various free traffic sources. Your traffic problem can be solved in a moment. Getting the attention of more people from various channels will drive more buyer traffic.

Until now, the power of SMS, email, social media push notifications, video sites, live streams, and messages from one single platform have still not been combined.

If you want traffic from multiple sources, you need to purchase different apps, that costs thousands of dollars. That is the reason software Prime comes into play.

PRIME is an info + software combo product that delivers unlimited high quality traffic from a 300 million traffic source for beginners, affiliate marketers, list builders & product owners to any link in any niche.

Now let's learn about this product to see how well it works in my Prime Review.

What is Prime Review?

Prime is software that allows you to search and post questions on Quora. It works in the background searching for relevant questions and posting answers with your links. Which can be an affiliate link for the product you're promoting or for any of your own service. This is how you're going to get traffic to your blog, to your pages through Quora.

https://anuradha561986.wordpress.com/

This is how the Prime Membership area looks like:

Prime Review – Features and Benefits

Prime is a cloud-based app that delivers unlimited top quality BUYER traffic from an untapped source of 300 million active monthly consumers.

Perfect for beginners, affiliates, eCommerce marketers, list builders & product owners to monetize ANY link in ANY niche on 100% autopilot.

Breakthrough 'artificial intelligence' app automates this MASSIVE untapped source of buyer traffic.

Free traffic in ANY niche

Set & forget: switch it on once, get free traffic for life

100% legal & ethical: one of the most trusted traffic platforms online

Instant authority for sky-high conversions from DFY original content with YOUR links posted by the app

No experience, no tech skills, no learning curve!

Vendor:

Company name – Digital page designs.

Name – Billy Darr, Finn Goswami, Justin Opay.

Location – London, U.K.

Prime Price and OTO's

Prime Front End: $12.95

<u>Visit My Official Website</u>

<u>PRIME</u> is is an info + software combo product that delivers unlimited high quality traffic from a 300 billion traffic

source for beginners, affiliate marketers, list builders & product owners to any link in any niche on complete automation cheaper (Free) and faster than any paid traffic method OR without the need of paying for ads, creating videos, creating your own products or any complicated setup.

This software searches and finds questions on Quora on total automation, it then posts your link for daily automated traffic, leads, optins and sales.

Upgrade 1 ($47/$27) – "Prime Unlimited Version"

Unlimited Everything – With this upgrade you will be able to Unlock more traffic by searching and answering unlimited questions on Quora on total automation + use it on unlimited accounts. Link/Url Shortener – Get your own link shortener for the offers you are promoting.

Upgrade 2 ($97/$47) – Prime Traffic Maximizer:

Use our Prime Traffic Maximizer Software and exponentially *double or triple* your traffic using our breakthrough cloud based technology.

Use this in combination with the Front end software of Prime and you will be exploding your traffic all without increasing your original traffic. It basically recycles your current traffic and creates more of it.Use any traffic source and exponentially reach more eyeballs.

You just copy a piece of simple code (takes 2 minutes) generated inside our cloud based interface to any page and it will automatically generate a notification inviting the user's visitors to share that content on social media and or through email in exchange for a gift.

Once the visitors share the content, the gift will be unlocked (which comes in form of a link where the person can access the gift) So, it will basically increase their results exponentially.

Upgrade 3 ($197) – High Ticket DFY Funnel + Limitless Traffic + Unlock Instagram & Twitter Pro Traffic Software

HUGE value once again here. Users get direct access to our adwords audience by placing pixels on our sales pages for the next 365 days. It doesn't stop there.... They also get access to Robin's personal High ticket Funnel (with complete email templates) that lands him several high ticket sales each month on autopilot. Access our Instagram & Twitter Pro Software for even more traffic.

Upgrade 4 ($197) – 3 Apps Products Resellers License Bundle

Combined developers rights to the software, resell rights + Access to 3 Of Robin's Best Converting Products. Buyers of this up-sell also get to sell Prime as if it was their own product and take away 100% commissions on the WHOLE funnel + 100% commissions on the entire funnel for 2 of Robin's latest products.

Prime – Pros & Cons?

Pros

–A.I. tech automates unlimited hands-free traffic in any niche

-No manual posting or maintenance needed

-No website, email list or social media needed

-Requires no previous tech skills or experience

Cons

– Can't find any so far

Honest Prime Review – Is It Worth Your Money?

Quora is a remarkable tool that can assist you enormously in your service.

It permits you to stay on top of necessary info that can significantly impact the success of your job.

It is also an incredible method to interact with other people and to build purposeful as well as durable partnerships.

Prime automates your usage of Quora and will save your valuable time of doing the work manually.

Visit My Official Website

Prime Bonus Package

Exclusive Bonus #1: 60 Mins Coaching Call

Exclusive Bonus #2: **7 Mins Sales Machine**

Exclusive Bonus #3: **Clickfunnels Alternative**

Exclusive Bonus #4: **How To Build Squeeze Pages**

Exclusive Bonus #5: **Make Money from TikTok**

Exclusive Bonus #6: **5 Instant Cash Strategies**

Exclusive Bonus #7: **How To Use Webinars In Your Business**

Exclusive Bonus #8: **Javascript Commission Bot PRO**

Exclusive Bonus #9: **BREAKOUT CODE + ALL OTO's**

Exclusive Bonus #10: **Make Money With Content Marketing**

Few previous good products created by this vendor are Orion – Dares You To Send 1 More Email, Krown – Deal Of The Week, Xtreme – Send 1 More Email, Hive, etc.

Simple three steps to start with Prime:

#1: Purchase a copy.

#2: Login and enter your link to get free traffic.

#3: Start getting traffic, leads, and sales.

What exactly will you get inside Prime?

The Prime software:

1-Click App Gets You Free Visitors in 23 seconds on autopilot. 300 Traffics sources across 7 channels such as email, SMS, social media, etc.

Autopilot system:

The Prime software gives you free buyer traffic, that generates passive money.

Simple and easy video tutorials:

The exact step-by-step video tutorials included no questions of being stuck anywhere.

Ready fire profit guide:

If you don't like to watch videos, they have a 60-second guide to show you the exact process.

Live chat customer support:

27/7 excellent live chat customer support is ready to solve any problem.

Real-life case study:

There are real-life case studies included to make you motivated and successful.

Call To Millions:

They have a 15 min onboarding call to ask questions and to find out where to get help & get results.

The live training:

It will be a live stream to show you how they use the primary software to obtain free traffic and sales in front of your eyes.

Pros:

In 1-click tap Into 300 Traffic Sources.

Enable the traffic system easily and earn money.

No technical knowledge or experience is required.

The 3-figure A-day case study included.

Get the real visitors who buy.

No need for any paid advertisements.

Get free traffic to sell today.

365-day money-back guarantee.

Cons:

No cons found so far.

Price details:

Front End: Prime– $17

The World's 1ˢᵗ 7-In-1 Multi-Channel Traffic App

Upsell 1: Prime – GoPro Edition – $39.

The GoPro Edition of Prime lets your customers unlock a further 3 channels including SEO, eCom & Affiliate Networks.

Upsell 2: Prime – Lazy Traffic DFY Edition – $197.

In this upgrade, our team aims to deliver Done-For-You traffic and Sales for your customers.

Upsell 3: Prime – Auto Edition – $39.

Your customers will be able to activate all the automation tools within Prime.

Upsell 4: Prime – Multi-Pay Edition – $39.

Your customers will be able to run 10 simultaneous campaigns for up to $517.70 per hour.

Upsell 5: Prime – GoXtreme – $67.

The unlimited edition of Prime lets your customers unlock unlimited campaigns, unlimited niches, unlimited traffic +

13 total traffic channels.

Vendor bonuses:

Get results in the first 5 minutes.

3 ways we bank fast with prime.

2021 year-end bundle.

Xmas cash kit.

How we scale prime to 10k/month.

<u>Visit My Official Website</u>

Conclusion:

Prime was developed for beginners, they don't just provide you with the software, but provide you the training, access to the support desk and live chat assistance to assist the members.

You can obtain free visitors to 7 various channels including social media, SMS, email, and more in just a single click of 300 distinct traffic sources.

A 365-day money refund guarantee is provided to Prime. It's a whole year to use Prime to traffic more than you want. Simply open here a ticket and they will return your money back if you're not pleased.

Only Two Simple steps to get my Bonuses:

Click here or any button above from this review page and purchase "Prime". Your bonuses will be sent to you through Warrior Plus's Purchases Dashboard. You will find a button "Access Affiliate Bonus" Inside Warrior Plus's Purchases Dashboard next to your Purchased product.

<u>Prime</u> Review Conclusion

I hope you find my *Prime Review* article helpful. If this is a software that you're interested in picking up then click the buttons on this page and get Prime with my free bonuses.

Grab your Prime license now completely risk free. Your investment is covered by their no hassle, money back guarantee.

<u>PRIME</u>

<u>Visit My Official Website</u>

Contents